FOCUS ON THE FAMILY

my Mom's
Sweet Influence

Photography by
Kathleen Francour

HARVEST HOUSE PUBLISHERS
Eugene, Oregon

MY MOM'S SWEET INFLUENCE
Text Copyright © 2001 by Focus on the Family®
Published by Harvest House Publishers
Eugene, Oregon 97402

Library of Congress Cataloging-in-Publication Data
Focus on the Family/ My mom's sweet influence : the heritage of a faithful mother/photography by Kathleen Francour.
  p. cm.
  ISBN 0-7369-0550-2
  1.Mothers. 2.Motherhood--Religious aspects--Christianity. I.Francour, Kathleen.

HQ759 .M989 2001
306.874'3--dc21   00-047116

Focus on the Family, headed by Dr. James Dobson, is an organization that reaches families with the message of God's love. Focus on the Family® is a registered trademark of Focus on the Family, Colorado Springs, CO 80995. For more information, please contact:

    Focus on the Family
    Colorado Springs, CO 80995
    1-800-A-Family (232-6459)
    www.family.org

Kathleen Francour's hand-tinted photographs reflect the old-fashioned values of home, family, love, loyalty, and friendship. The photography in this book is copyrighted by Kathleen Francour and may not be used without permission of the photographer. For more information, please contact:

    Kathleen Francour Photography & Design
    P.O. Box 1206
    Carefree, AZ 85377

Photographic printing by Isgo Lepejian

Design and production by Koechel Peterson and Associates, Minneapolis, Minnesota

Harvest House Publishers has made every effort to trace the ownership of all poems and quotes. In the event of a question arising from the use of a poem or quote, we regret any error made and will be pleased to make the necessary correction in future editions of this book.

Acknowledgments

"It's Never Too Late," copyright © by Mary Pierce. Used by permission.
"Prayer Warrior," copyright © by Shirley Dobson. Used by permission.
"Building Memorials on a Firm Foundation," copyright © by Lynda Hunter. Used by permission.
"Growing a Grateful Heart," copyright © by Ann Hibbard. Used by permission.

Scripture quotations are taken from the Holy Bible, New International Version®, Copyright © 1973, 1978, 1984 by the International Bible Society. Used by permission of Zondervan Publishing House.

Printed in Italy

01 02 03 04 05 06 07 08 09 10 / PBI / 10 9 8 7 6 5 4 3 2 1

SHE IS CLOTHED WITH
STRENGTH AND DIGNITY;
SHE CAN LAUGH AT THE DAYS
TO COME.
SHE SPEAKS WITH WISDOM,
AND FAITHFUL INSTRUCTION
IS ON HER TONGUE.
SHE WATCHES OVER THE
AFFAIRS OF HER HOUSEHOLD
AND DOES NOT EAT THE
BREAD OF IDLENESS.
HER CHILDREN ARISE AND CALL
HER BLESSED.

The Book of Proverbs

A Mother's Journey

The young mother set her foot on the path of life.

"Is the way long?" she asked.

And her guide said, "Yes, and the way is hard. And you will be old before you reach the end of it. But the end will be better than the beginning."

But the young mother was happy, and she would not believe that anything could be better than these years. So she played with her children, and gathered flowers for them along the way, and played with them in the clear streams. And the sun shone on them, and life was good, and the young mother cried, "Nothing will be lovelier than this."

Then night came, and a storm, and the path was dark, and the children shook with fear and cold, and the mother drew them close and covered them. And the children said, "Mother, we are not afraid, for you are near, and no harm can come."

And the mother said, "This is better than the brightness of day, for I have taught my children courage."

And the morning came, and there was a hill ahead, and the children climbed and grew weary, and the mother was weary, but at all times she said to the children, "A little patience and we are there."

So the children climbed, and when they reached the top they said, "Mother, we would not have done it without you." And the mother, when she lay down that night, looked up at the stars and said, "This is a better day than the last, for my children have learned fortitude in the face of difficulty. Yesterday, I gave them courage. Today, I have given them strength."

And the next day came strange clouds that darkened the earth. Clouds of war and hate and evil, and the children groped and stumbled, and the

MY MOTHER WAS THE SOURCE FROM

WHICH I DERIVED THE GUIDING

PRINCIPLES OF MY LIFE.

John Wesley

mother said, "Look up. Lift your eyes to the Light." And the children looked and saw above the clouds an Everlasting Glory, and it guided them and brought them beyond the darkness. And that night, the mother said, "This is the best day of all, for I have shown my children God."

And the days went on, and the weeks and the months and the years, and the mother grew older. But her children were strong and walked with courage. And when the way was hard, they helped their mother. And when the way was rough, they lifted her.

And at last she came to a hill, and beyond she could see a shining road and golden gates flung wide. And the mother said, "I have reached the end of my journey. And now I know that the end is better than the beginning, for my children can walk alone and their children after them."

And the children said, "You will always walk with us, Mother, even when you have gone through the gates."

And they stood and watched her as she went on alone, and the gates closed after her. And they said, "We cannot see her, but she is with us still. A mother like ours is more than a memory. She is a living presence."

—TEMPLE BAILEY

ALWAYS MAKE TIME FOR GOD

I was one of seven children, and we lived a very busy life on a dairy farm. And yet in spite of all this, my mom still found time to give us a little special attention and encouragement in whatever we attempted.

She faithfully took us to church every Sunday, wanting to instill within us her faith and trust in the God she loved. I will always remember the open Bible on the table, and how nightly, she would read from it no matter how weary she was from the day's duties.

She'll always remain in my memory as a godly, loving, and kind mother.

—KAREN MILLSAP

It's Never Too Late

Be thankful for

our mothers,

for they love

with a higher love...

from the power

God has given,

and the strength

from up above.

Jill Lemming

We watched God draw Mama closer and closer. And at age 85, she changed her mind about Him. When a wise pastor explained how she could open her heart to God, she did. After they prayed together, she said, "Everything is different now. I felt empty before. I'm not empty anymore."

And now she prays. Just as Mama was leaving our home on a recent visit, our puppy ran away, disappearing into the woods behind our house. I fumed about this rebellious pup who bolts at every opportunity; I imagined the worst. Mama, familiar with the ways of the prodigal, looked me in the eye and asked, "Where's your faith?"

My faith? Swift and sure conviction swept over me. This little woman was suddenly a spiritual giant towering over me. Where was my faith?

"I'll pray about this," she said, patting my arm, lifting my burden with her touch. My mother was going to pray. Everything would be all right.

Within five minutes of her departure, the dog was back in the house, happily wolfing down her dinner. When I passed along the good news later on the phone, Mama said, "Boy, He works fast! I talked to Him just as we left your driveway!" As I hung up, the words to an old Southern gospel song came to mind, "When Mama prayed, Heaven paid attention."

Mama looked for 85 years and never found anything in this world to fill the emptiness only God can fill. She taught us her best lesson yet—it's never too late to change your mind and accept God's invitation to be His child.

—MARY PIERCE

WHEN MAMA PRAYED

I walked in the garden of roses

At the closing of the day,

In the shadows I saw my mother

And I watched as she knelt there to pray.

And the words from her lips were so dear to my heart

As she talked to the Father above.

With childlike plea, yet sincere as could be,

She prayed from a heart full of love.

She spoke of her love for neighbors,

And her friends were like jewels so rare.

Yet she trusted each beautiful friendship

To the Heavenly Father up there.

And then her soft voice became broken,

As she spoke with a pride all her own.

She was asking the Heavenly Father

To bless all her family and home.

As twilight surrounded the garden,

Each rose seemed more lovely and fair.

And the stars shining down from the heavens

Seemed so near to our garden of prayer.

And then Mother spoke the name "Jesus"

And, "Thank You, dear God, for your Son."

'Twas then I could feel the presence

Of God through the Holy One.

The rose garden long has been faded,

As all earthly things must decay.

And Mother's with Jesus in Heaven,

So long now since she went away.

I'm so glad that God's prayer line is still open,

And that Mother taught me how to pray.

For I know she is patiently waiting

Until we meet her in Heaven that day.

—CREOLA KNIFLEY GOODE

And IT BECAME A HOUSEHOLD CUSTOM,

FOR THE MOTHER WAS A BORN SINGER. THE

FIRST SOUND IN THE MORNING WAS HER

VOICE AS SHE WENT ABOUT THE HOUSE

SINGING LIKE A LARK, AND THE LAST SOUND

AT NIGHT WAS THE SAME CHEERY SOUND,

FOR THE GIRLS NEVER GREW TOO OLD FOR

THAT FAMILIAR LULLABY.

Louisa May Alcott
LITTLE WOMEN

PRAYER WARRIOR

When I was a girl, my loving mother sent me to a little evangelical church where I learned about Jesus. Right from the start, I developed a personal relationship with Him and knew He heard me when I prayed.

When I was eight years old, I would go into my little bedroom, close the door, kneel by my bed, and talk to the Lord not only about my present anxieties and longings, but also about my future.

My husband, Jim, also learned to pray at an early age. His father was a great man of prayer, and his mother was a godly woman, but he says his grandmother and great-grandmother

had the greatest spiritual impact on him. They talked about the Lord continually and took every opportunity to teach him about Jesus. Jim was still very young when both these women died, but he is quick to talk about the profound effect they had on him.

He especially likes to tell a story from his boyhood. One day when he was five, he was standing in the backyard with "Nanny," his great-grandmother. Pearl Harbor had just been bombed, and the United States was at war. A fighter plane flew over, and Nanny said, "Oh, we have to pray for that man up there."

Jim asked, "Why, what's wrong with him?"

Nanny explained that the pilot was someone important to God, a man with a family who loved him, and they should pray for his safety. It was her way of bringing prayer and spiritual matters into everyday life.

—SHIRLEY DOBSON

Then ma began to sway gently in the comfortable rocking chair...And ma sang, softly and sweetly:

"There's a happy land,
Far, far away,
Where saints in glory stand,
Bright, bright as day.

"Oh, to hear the angels sing,
Glory to the lord, our king—"

Laura didn't know that she had gone to sleep. She thought the shining angels began to sing with ma, and she lay listening to their heavenly singing...

Laura Ingalls Wilder
Little House on the Prairie

Standing Tall With Christ

My mother has faced a lot of hardships in her life. But, through it all, she has trusted in our Lord Jesus Christ to stand by her. This never-ending love of the Lord has been the driving force behind her all of her 75 years. She has loved me unconditionally throughout my life and has allowed me to know that Jesus is alive and that He loves me. Because of her tireless effort, throughout her lifetime, she has brought joy to so many friends and relatives. Thanks, Mom, for being the inspiration I need.

—BECKY MURRAY

God gave us mothers to emulate Him
By providing us an anchor,
By believing in us when others don't,
By comforting us in difficult times,
By drawing us to the source of life.

God gave us mothers to guide us,
By setting a godly example,
By teaching us to be a friend,
By showing us how to grow,
By extending a helping hand.

God gave us mothers to inspire us,
To just be there for us,
To keep us in the straight and narrow way,
To love us above all else.

God gave us mothers to nurture us
Until we could draw our own
nourishment from Him,
To open His Word to us until
we could dig in for ourselves,
To pray for us at all times.

God gave us mothers because He knew
We needed someone to answer our questions,
To teach us responsibility,
To lead us to our Savior,
To help us walk in truth.

God gave us a mother because He knew
She'd appreciate our uniqueness.
He knew she'd value us.
He knew she'd willingly give herself to us.
He knew she'd excel in patience.

God gave us mothers to walk with us
Through our youth,
So that we could become
All that He wants us to be.

—STELLA CALLOWAY

Building Memorials on a Firm Foundation

My mom and dad became Christians when I was six months old. From that point, they sought to learn everything they could about God and to raise my eldest sister and me and six younger siblings to know the Lord.

Despite my parents' newfound reliance on Christ, things were never easy. We battled financial hardships, health problems, and other difficulties. Yet today, I can observe the lives of each of my brothers and sisters, as well as my own life, and see memorials that show how God has remained faithful.

My parents blazed a trail for me in their walk with God.

One day at a time, they learned to call on the Lord and rely on Him in all circumstances. They were not fortunate enough to have had parents who knew this faith, but I was. Knowing I could ask for God's help in everything—from a spelling test in school to the major decisions that would channel my future—became a way of life for me.

As a second-generation Christian now raising a third, my challenge is the same as it was for my parents. When God teaches me that He is a God who provides by making our finances stretch, I share this fact with the kids. When He shows me His power to heal by touching the fevered brow of one of my children, they discover this too. When they see me go to Him for wisdom and guidance and then watch Him come through, my children learn to do the same in their own lives. And when they ask me, "What does this memorial mean?" I don't hesitate to tell them.

—LYNDA HUNTER

HONOR YOUR FATHER AND YOUR
MOTHER, AS THE LORD YOUR GOD HAS
COMMANDED YOU, SO THAT YOU MAY
LIVE LONG AND THAT IT MAY GO WELL
WITH YOU IN THE LAND THE LORD
YOUR GOD IS GIVING YOU.

The Book of Deuteronomy

Growing a Grateful Heart

i still remember my mother's shrieks of excitement when she found a lost item after praying for its recovery. "Thank You, Lord Jesus!" she would exclaim. Nothing was too trivial to bring to God in prayer, and when He answered, she openly praised Him.

I always thank God for a loving Christian mother who taught me that "Every good gift comes from God." She reminded us constantly that He provides food, safety, health, family, and friends—in addition to all the spiritual blessings that belong to those who are in Christ. Her example of thankfulness has had a profound effect on me. Even more, it has shown me the importance of keeping that legacy alive by handing it down to my own children.

—ANN HIBBARD

A MOTHER IS THE TRUEST FRIEND WE HAVE,
WHEN TRIALS, HEAVY AND SUDDEN, FALL UPON
US; WHEN ADVERSITY TAKES THE PLACE OF
PROSPERITY; WHEN FRIENDS WHO REJOICE WITH
US IN OUR SUNSHINE, DESERT US WHEN
TROUBLES THICKEN AROUND US, STILL WILL
SHE CLING TO US, AND ENDEAVOR BY HER KIND
PRECEPTS AND COUNSELS TO DISSIPATE THE
CLOUDS OF DARKNESS, AND CAUSE PEACE TO
RETURN TO OUR HEARTS.

Washington Irving

THE GIFT OF PATIENCE

If patience is one of the fruits of the Spirit, then my mother has an orchard of it growing lushly in her heart. She is the most patient woman I have ever known. She gave birth to five children in five years…and then four-and-a-half years later, had one more. Six little kids in a crowd around her must have tested her patience a lot, but I never saw it.

Growing up, I grieved over my own lack of patience. I have a tendency to rush through life with too much on my plate, and I quickly become impatient at the least hindrance in my day or schedule. I often wish I had my mother's ability to relate to people and events around me. Then, one day, I

received a revelation…an outside observation from another mother in my life, my grandmother.

We were shopping in a busy mall a few years ago just after Christmas. The aisles were cluttered with people for the post-holiday sales. My job was to occupy my niece so that my sister had some time to shop. Like any good aunt, I had been sneaking her candy throughout the morning and noticed she was becoming quite sticky. I knelt down among the fuss and bustle and took a few moments to clean her up. I was having a good time tickling her and cajoling her into cooperating with me when my grandmother said, "Kim, you have the patience of a saint." Her words took me by surprise.

Now, I know that not many people would say that about me. But my grandmother saw something in my life that I couldn't see. She saw in me the spiritual legacy of patience I had inherited from my mom…fruit from a woman walking

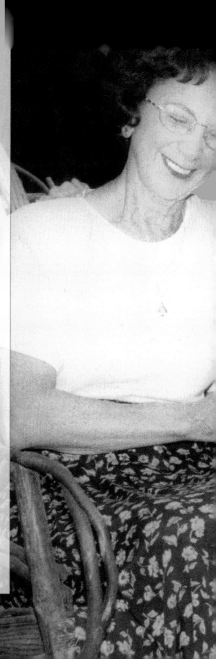

close to God that was passed on to her daughter. Her godly example had penetrated my being and shaped my own actions almost without my being aware of it. The patience and love that so permeates her character reached through me to bless others in our family.

I think there are many other good things she has bequeathed to my life that are invisible to me…but not to others. I'm sure that is true for all of us. Godly parents can have a tremendous influence on their children even years after the children have left home. My grandmother showed me that I have one little sapling of patience. Thankfully, I will start with that, and maybe someday an orchard will grow lushly in my heart. Thanks, Mom, for planting the seed.

—KIMBERLY MOORE

A Mother's Tribute

Nurtures, teaches, loves, protects.
And when necessary, she corrects.
In my happiness, she too will rejoice
Sharing my excitement, she lifts her voice.

Excruciatingly, she feels my pain
Cries in my sorrow, burns with my shame.
Wanting only what is best for me
When my paths are cluttered
And my eyes don't see.

Is this the pain of which God spoke,
When fellowship in Eden broke?
From the Lord comes
her strength to persevere
Lines of communication
kept open and clear.

Pleading my case through
prayerful intercession.
Prodded along at His Spirit's suggestion
Asking for wisdom so she will know
When to hold tight
And when to let go.

Preparing me to live
in a world of choice
To stop and listen for His voice
Words of encouragement
lovingly spoken
Silently tell me the
door is left open.

There when she's needed,
Steadfast and pleasing,
Her shoulder so soft,
and love never ceasing
To whom has God granted
this position of trust?
To mother who gathers her
treasures in a place without rust.

—SUSAN GOLDRA

THANK YOU, MOTHER, FOR
MY YESTERDAYS AS YOU
HELD ME TIGHT IN THE PALM
OF YOUR HAND, AND MAY
MY TOMORROWS BE SPENT
WITH GOD SAFE IN THE
PALM OF HIS HAND.

Alda Ellis

That best academy,

a mother's knee.

James Russell Lowell

LEARNING BY EXAMPLE

*M*om, thank you for giving to your five children the tools we needed to be successful. You didn't send us to the most expensive schools for an education. We didn't wear expensive store-bought clothes. We didn't travel worldwide seeing all there is to see. And we didn't join every club and activity that was offered. The tools that you gave us were watching you pray and read your Bible every day, hearing you comfort a friend, and seeing you talk gently to a patient in the nursing home. And watching you love, and yes, biblically submit to your husband.

The world may not think being a mother is the most important thing you have done in your life, but you made an eternal impact on your five children to love and serve the Lord. And now we are passing on those tools needed to be successful to your 17 grandchildren.

—DOREEN BORQUIST

THE *N*EXT GENERATION

*M*y mom did not go to church when she was growing up. In fact, she did not give her life to Christ until she was 30 years old and pregnant with me, the fourth of her five children. When she chose to follow Christ, she did so with everything she had. It is because of this that I am in awe of this woman of God. She understood that becoming a Christian is the first step—not the only step. My early memories are of a mother who first prayed with me, then taught me to pray. Her life is a reflection of her faith and, while she is not likely

to stand on a soapbox and preach, she has helped countless people see that her God is a loving God. She is a servant in the true, Christ-like sense of the word. Her love and encouragement, her commitment to grow and to know God better each day, are all reasons that I am serving the Lord faithfully today.

—STACY HAUSLER

A MOTHER'S LOVE IS NEW EVERY DAY.

GOD BLESS OUR FAITHFUL GOOD MOTHERS.